Original title:
Rocket Ship Rhymes

Copyright © 2025 Creative Arts Management OÜ
All rights reserved.

Author: Miriam Kensington
ISBN HARDBACK: 978-1-80567-802-1
ISBN PAPERBACK: 978-1-80567-923-3

Starlit Journeys

A cat in a hat, flew high in the night,
On a quest for some cheese, oh what a sight!
With a wink and a grin, he soared through the stars,
Chasing dreams and some Mars candy bars.

In a ship made of cheese, they danced with the moon,
Bouncing on comets, they sang a sweet tune.
With laughter and joy, they zoomed through the sky,
As asteroids giggled, "Oh my, oh my!"

Celestial Melodies

A dog with a trombone played jazzy delight,
On a journey to Pluto, oh what a night!
He tooted and howled, with stars in his eyes,
As aliens cheered, "What a clever surprise!"

With a jolt and a jig, stars twinkled with glee,
Dancing in rhythm, like waves in the sea.
They twirled and they whirled in a cosmic affair,
Making melodies rare, floating soft through the air.

Blast Off Ballads

A penguin with dreams set his sights on the skies,
Wearing goggles and goggles, with wide-open eyes.
He flapped and he flailed, trying hard to take flight,
Until he found joy in the starry twilight.

With a whoosh and a bounce, he landed with flair,
On a planet of marshmallows, fluffy and rare.
He munched and he crunched, made a home in a dome,
And wrote funny songs 'bout his sugary home.

Orbiting Echoes

A squirrel on a quest found a jet made of nuts,
He painted it bright, and he gathered his chuts.
To the rings of old Saturn, he zipped and he zapped,
While space squirrels laughed, they happily snapped.

With acorns as fuel, they danced on the breeze,
Making trails of light, like sweet cosmic cheese.
They winked at the planets, shared jokes with a grin,
In a universe chuckling, where adventure begins.

Tales from the Twilight Zone

In a land where strange things fly,
A cat may just give pizza a try.
The clocks tick loud, the sun turns blue,
Dancing cows sing songs to you.

Bright purple trees with candy bark,
And squirrels ride unicycles in the park.
UFOs serve ice cream cones,
While aliens borrow our garden gnomes.

Radiance of the Astral Realm

Stars giggle as they light the sky,
While space whales leap and soar up high.
Jellybeans rain from clouds of fluff,
And planets play tag—oh, that's quite enough!

An astronaut wears socks that glow,
While comets play hide and seek below.
The moon sings lullabies soft and sweet,
While stardust dances under our feet.

Melodies Among the Moons

Singing moons with faces round,
Play jazz with comets as they bound.
Asteroids tap their tiny feet,
Creating rhythms, oh so neat.

In this realm where laughter swells,
Space mice ring the cosmic bells.
Galaxies spin in playful flight,
As harmonies sing us into the night.

Verses Written in the Dark Matter

In dark matter, where shadows grin,
Curly fries are served with a spin.
Gravity pulls you for a dance,
As wiggly stars take a chance.

Gigantic jellyfish drift and sway,
Giving hugs to asteroids at play.
Aliens draw with glowing pens,
While all the silence just pretends.

Lightyear Lyrics

In a galaxy not so far,
An alien plays a guitar.
With strings made of spaghetti,
He plays tunes that are quite confetti.

The stars all twinkle in delight,
As he strums under moonlight.
Dancing moons join the tune,
While planets sway in a cartoon.

Echoes of the Universe.

A comet sneezed and left a trail,
That made the stars all laugh and wail.
They said, "Oh bless you, speedy friend!"
And giggled on until the end.

A satellite lost its way one day,
It tried to find the Milky Way.
But its GPS was out of whack,
Now it parks in a space junk stack.

Soaring Through Starlit Verses

A spaceship filled with silly mice,
Made sure their seats were soft as rice.
They flew past Mars with cheese to eat,
And had a party—what a feat!

The astronauts wore hats of cheese,
Floating around with perfect ease.
They danced with asteroids in the sky,
As cosmic giggles drifted by.

Cosmic Dreams Aflutter

A robot tripped on asteroid rocks,
Chasing space kittens in cute socks.
They played hide and seek in a star,
Hiding near Jupiter's candy bar.

Galaxies winked with glee and cheer,
As supernovas danced near.
With a sprinkle of stardust in the air,
Who knew space could be such a fair?

Twinkling Tales

Up in the sky, so high and bright,
Stars are having a giggling night.
Planets twist in a silly dance,
Comets zoom in a sparkling trance.

Moon winks down with a twinkling gleam,
While the sun launches a cheesy beam.
Galaxies chime with a bouncy tune,
While asteroids play hide and seek with the moon.

Hubble's Harmony

In a telescope's gaze, the stars peek out,
Singing their songs without a doubt.
Asteroids juggle in a cosmic art,
While black holes pull at the heart.

Shooting stars slide down rainbows bright,
Tickling the space with pure delight.
Nebulas swirl, painting the sky,
Galactic laughter, oh my, oh my!

Celestial Sonatas

Planets gather for a grand old fête,
Listening to the Milky Way's sweet fate.
Jupiter plays the bongo drums,
While Venus shakes to the silly hums.

Martian mice break out in dance,
Twisting and turning, they prance.
Uranus jokes, as Saturn grins wide,
Cosmic merriment can't be denied.

Flight of the Cosmic Dream

Blast off the ground, into the sky,
Where zany aliens comically fly.
Whirlwinds of laughter dance with grace,
As colorful ships spin in space.

Gravity giggles, pulling us near,
While astronauts chuckle without fear.
Stars in spacesuits hold hands so tight,
Gliding through a silly starry night.

Lunar Lullabies

In pajamas so bright, they soar through the night,
With winks from the moon, oh what a delight!
They sip fizzy drinks, floating light as a feather,
While planets all giggle, and dance in the weather.

Stars play tag with a wink and a shout,
While cheeky old comets play peek-a-boo out!
A tumble of giggles, a sprinkle of cheer,
In dreamland they frolic, with nothing to fear.

Nebula Narratives

A cloud made of candy drifts through the skies,
With licorice trails and sweet sugar pies.
Asteroids munch on the marshmallow treats,
While moonbeams burst into silly, loud beats.

Once a star tried to juggle, oh what a mess!
With meteors rolling in a cosmic dress.
Laughter erupted, the cosmos awake,
In this candy land, they all take a break.

Stellar Stanzas

In the land of the stars, what a comical sight,
Where alien critters dance under the light.
They wear silly hats made of glitter and foam,
And sing out loud, "Let's make this our home!"

Galaxies twirl with a flick and a spin,
Whispering jokes about where they've been.
With laughter that echoes through cosmic winds,
Even the black holes smile as the fun begins.

Comet's Tale

A comet named Fred zoomed past with a grin,
With sparkles and laughter, he invited them in.
They played hide-and-seek behind Saturn's rings,
And told silly stories of extraterrestrial things.

Then Fred, with a wink, did a loop-de-loop dance,
The planets all chuckled, entranced in a trance.
They twirled and they whirled, all around the sky,
In a carnival atmosphere, oh my, oh my!

Meditations in the Astral Plane

Floating high up in space,
Came a squirrel with a funny face.
He tried to catch a galaxy star,
But ended up tangled in a guitar.

Thinking deep about his fate,
He mused, 'This could be first-rate!'
But the stars just laughed and twinkled,
As the guitar strings lightly crinkled.

He jumped on a comet so swift,
Said, 'This ride is quite the gift!'
But soon he found he'd lost his grip,
And spun around on a fleeting trip.

As his furry tail spun around,
He whispered, 'I'm lost, but I'm not bound!'
With each twist, he grinned all along,
For laughter echoed in the cosmic throng.

The Wisdom of Wandering Galaxies

A clown once sailed on a space breeze,
Chasing stardust under cosmic trees.
He wore a hat, two sizes too big,
And danced on planets, oh so sprig!

He asked a moon about its cheese,
The moon just chuckled, hard to please.
'It's not for eating, just for show,
Silly clown, don't you know?'

Through swirling worlds, he found a friend,
A talking comet who wouldn't bend.
They juggled meteors, made a mess,
And laughed at cosmic, glorious success.

But soon the clown felt something odd,
His funny shoes began to prod.
'Let's bounce to Earth for one last joke,
And leave the vastness in our cloak!'

Celestial Ink Across the Galaxy

A spaceship flew with purple ink,
Spraying stars while squirrels wink.
It painted comets in a line,
Creating smiles with each design.

An astronaut with a goofy grin,
Decided it was time to spin.
He painted half a moon bright pink,
Leaving astronomers to think.

With a brush made of starlight beams,
He crafted clouds and rainbow dreams.
Each swirl and twirl brought out a cheer,
In every quadrant far and near.

But he slipped on a cloud, rolled away,
Laughing loud, he'd found his play.
'Next time I'll stick to painting skies,
And maybe draw a friend who flies!'

Cosmic Calligraphy of the Heavens

In the universe where words take flight,
A quill wrote everything in sight.
It danced among the rings of stars,
Making scribbles and silly bars.

It stretched from moon to distant sun,
Creating poems, oh what fun!
Each letter twinkled, vibrant, bright,
As planets giggled at the sight.

A dancing word took form and spun,
While laughing orbits had their fun.
The brush made of gravitational glee,
Wrote tales of space for all to see.

But the quill got tangled in a joke,
And wrapped around a passing bloke.
They soared together, laughing high,
In a script that floated through the sky.

A Journey Beyond the Eventide

With wobbly legs, we take to the sky,
A goofy grin, oh me, oh my!
The stars will giggle as we zoom past,
On this silly ride, we'll have a blast.

We dodge the moon and swirl with glee,
Like ducks in a pond, we frolic so free!
With candy clouds and marshmallow beams,
We sail through the cosmos, living our dreams.

Quatrains in the Quiet of Space

In a tin can, we drift in delight,
With twisty straws sipping starlight!
Zero gravity makes us float,
Like fish in a bowl, we dance and gloat.

Galactic hiccups from all the snacks,
Wobbling paths on our silly tracks!
Bouncing astronauts with silly hats,
Creating a ruckus—oh, imagine that!

The Fabric of Dreams Unraveled

Stitching together a quilt of the night,
With giggles sewn into every right!
Cats in spacesuits chase glittering tails,
While penguins fly with sparkling sails.

Monkeys in orbit play tag with stars,
While ice cream comets race candy bars!
On cotton candy clouds, we'll swirl around,
In this whimsical realm where joy abounds.

Emissaries of Cosmic Thought

Shooting stars wear party hats so tall,
As we bounce and boogie, we're having a ball!
Galactic travel at the speed of fun,
With silly antics till the day is done.

We swap our giggles with Martian friends,
As tickles and chuckles through the ether sends!
In a universe where laughter reigns,
Our cosmic capers break all the chains.

Orbiting Imaginations

In a spaceship made of cheese,
We zoom past stars with ease.
Galaxies wag their tails,
As we spin around in flailing sails.

Planets sing a silly tune,
Jupiter dances with a cartoon.
Neptune's hat is quite the sight,
While Saturn spins in pure delight.

With aliens sharing goofy jokes,
And cosmic winds that tickle folks.
Our laughter echoes far and wide,
As we sail through the starry tide.

Each asteroid's a bouncy ball,
Skipping 'round like a seven-foot tall.
In this wacky space parade,
Every moment's a jolly escapade.

Flight of the Comet's Tale

On a comet made of candy bright,
We zoom through space with all our might.
Trailing sparkles like confetti,
Our laughter's bubbling, warm and petty.

Zipping past a moonlit cake,
We take a break for fun's own sake.
Aliens join for a silly snack,
As we giggle and plot our track.

With a whirl and a twirl, we spin and glide,
Racing past our galactic guide.
Stars twinkle with a teasing grin,
As we launch ourselves for another win.

Our comet's tail is quite the sight,
Shining bright in the starry night.
With each bounce and silly cheer,
We spread joy throughout the sphere.

Rhyme Beyond the Milky Way

In a spaceship filled with rhyme,
We skedaddle through space and time.
With words that tickle and delight,
We create a party every night.

Dancing with stars in a cosmic waltz,
Galactic giggles are never a fault.
Planets chuckle, asteroids grin,
As we spin with a joyful spin.

Through the void, we fly with glee,
Chasing dreams as bright as can be.
Comets join the zany game,
In this universe of endless fame.

With rhymes that bounce from star to star,
Every moment is bizarre and ajar.
In the Milky Way's twinkling embrace,
We spread our laughter all over space!

A Dance on Cosmic Strings

On strings of light, we skip and prance,
In a universe of joyful dance.
Gravity pulls but we break free,
With a twirl and a wink, it's pure history.

Stars play marbles in the expanse,
While we juggle planets at a glance.
Galaxies giggle with every whirl,
As we twirl like a cosmic pearl.

With a sprinkle of stardust and cheer,
We float about without any fear.
The milky waves keep our hearts light,
As we laugh 'til it's morning bright.

In this celestial ball of delight,
Every step is a spark in the night.
So let's dance on these cosmic strings,
And revel in the joy that space sings.

Celestial Canvas of Rhymes

In space a cat yawns loud,
Chasing comets, feeling proud.
An alien sneezes, oh my dear,
A solar flare brings laughter near.

The moon wears socks, oh so bright,
Dancing with stars in the night.
Mars tries to juggle, what a sight,
As planets giggle with pure delight.

Asteroids play a bumpy game,
While Venus giggles, never tame.
A cosmic joke is always told,
By shooting stars, so brave and bold.

Galaxies twist in silly shapes,
With gleeful laughs and playful vapes.
The universe bursts in a cheer,
Where funny rhymes just disappear!

Through the Looking Glass of Time

A clock with legs runs around,
Ticking jokes are what he's found.
Time wears glasses, quite absurd,
Reading jokes without a word.

The future laughs with silly glee,
Past tickles us, can't you see?
Every second has a grin,
As moments dance and spin within.

Mirrorballs reflect the fun,
Time is hectic, always on the run.
Past and present make a bet,
Who has the silliest silhouette?

Soon we shall fly, oh what a race,
Time's a joker, keeping pace.
In reality's grand old mime,
We find ourselves, lost in rhyme.

Lyricism Among the Stars

A star wrote lyrics on the moon,
With melodies that made us swoon.
Comets join in with a beat,
Creating grooves that's hard to beat.

Planets croon in perfect time,
Singing notes that sound like crime.
A black hole hums a deep, dark tune,
While astronauts dance under the moon.

Shooting stars can't hold their glee,
As they swirl in harmony, you see.
Every twinkle holds a song,
In space where funny feelings throng.

Astro-bands rock with sparkly flair,
Galactic giggles fill the air.
With every note, a cosmic tease,
Stars unite, we laugh with ease.

Vibrations of Celestial Harmony

Space is buzzing, can you hear?
Cosmic laughter rings so clear.
Black holes whisper silly tunes,
While planets dance like silly loons.

Asteroids strum their rocky bones,
Platinum comets make funny tones.
The sun winks with a cheeky glow,
As stardust blooms in nature's show.

Nebulas swirl with a vibrant cheer,
Each color sends a giggle near.
Galaxies trap a playful sound,
And launch it far, where joy is found.

Einstein grins from distant stars,
Astronauts chuckle, wielding guitars.
In the universe's crazy spree,
Harmonies spark wild jubilee!

Whispers of the Galactic Breeze

In a world where stars can giggle,
Planets wobble and do a jiggle.
Asteroids dance in a silly haze,
Comets twirl in a starry maze.

Aliens wear the silliest hats,
Floating by on their chubby cats.
Shooting stars play tag at night,
Laughing softly, what a sight!

Space is filled with quirky cheers,
Echoing through the cosmic spheres.
Gravity plays tricks like a clown,
Making astronauts tumble down.

So if you're lost in the night sky,
Just look for the laughter, oh my, oh my!
Each twinkle sings a funny tune,
In this wacky cosmic maroon.

Celestial Journeys in Rhyme

Zoom past planets all aglow,
With space cows saying, "Moo! Let's go!"
Nebulas swirl like cotton candy,
As Martian dogs bark, "Is it handy?"

Galaxies spin with a magical twist,
In a vacuum where you can't resist.
Cosmic surfboards riding the breeze,
Sliding through stars with greatest ease.

Comets wear their best parade gear,
While space whales sing, loud and clear.
Astro-bunnies hop high and wide,
In this joyful, interstellar ride.

So buckle up, let's take a dip,
In the silly cosmic, laughter trip.
With each star that twinkles and shines,
Join the fun in these rhyming lines.

Starlit Stanzas on a Silver Path

Dancing across the dark blue void,
Silly space suits, oh boy, oh boy!
Stars are winking, playing peek-a-boo,
Singing tunes that are funny and new.

Jupiter jokes about its size,
While Saturn sports its blingy ties.
Planets gossip in a playful tease,
Bouncing about with the greatest ease.

Uranus chuckles at the tales told,
Of adventures in the galaxy bold.
The Milky Way giggles with delight,
As starlight sparkles throughout the night.

So take a trip on this rhyming spree,
Where laughter floats like a cosmic sea.
Every verse a twirl, every line a dance,
Join the fun in this stellar romance.

Adventures in Infinity's Embrace

In a rocket with a squeaky chair,
Zooming off without a care!
Stars throw parties in their glow,
While asteroid siblings put on a show.

Zany aliens play in the sand,
Building castles that are just so grand.
Meteor showers rain down confetti,
And cosmic kittens are always ready.

Fuzzy planets offer you a snack,
As comets whistle, racing back.
Each orbit spins a giggling tale,
Where even the black holes wobble and flail.

So grab your gear, jump in right now,
Join our cosmic fun, take a bow.
With laughter echoing through the night,
Let's explore the universe, what a sight!

The Poetry of Flight

In a cockpit made of jellybeans,
We'll zoom past all those crazy scenes.
With marshmallow clouds and soda streams,
We'll giggle loud, or so it seems.

The radar's broken—oh what a joke!
It says we're flying over a giant oak.
Blasting through space as we happily poke,
Chasing down a star that's gone up in smoke.

A squirrel in a helmet gives us a wave,
And a comet shoots by, so bold and brave.
Our laughter echoes, a sweet, sweet rave,
Creating a rhythm that we all crave.

As we land on the moon with a crunchy plop,
We bounce around, and we never stop.
With zero-gravity dancing, we flip and flop,
In this silly world, you just can't drop.

Constellation Crescendo

Amidst the stars, we twirl and spin,
Searching for a place where we can win.
With giggles that shimmer and huge grins,
Every new adventure, we dive right in.

The Big Dipper plays a silly tune,
While a grumpy old star starts to swoon.
Twinkling lights dance under the moon,
Singing with joy, we're all immune!

A pop quiz on who ate the last snack,
The Martian claims it was a sneak attack.
With cosmic confetti; there's no lack,
In this starry chaos, we all unpack.

We draw in the sky with candy floss,
Twirling around like we're at a toss.
Chasing cosmic wishes, we're the boss,
In this playful galaxy, we're never at a loss.

Cosmic Cadence

A spaceship built from paper and dreams,
Gliding past Saturn with silly beams.
Singing out loud, we can hear the screams,
Of aliens giggling in starry teams.

Through asteroid belts, we weave and laugh,
Counting the seconds like a funny calf.
Floating along in a bubble bath,
As space-time bends, we join the daft.

Rockets made of marshmallows, puffed and bright,
Bouncing like balls in the deep of night.
With gravity forgetting its own plight,
We dance with the stars, what a delight!

In a cosmic parade, we shout, "Hooray!"
We're the funniest crew, that's what they say.
With light-up shoes, we lead the way,
In this wacky universe, we'll forever stay!

Odyssey of the Stars

Zooming through space on a donut ship,
With frosting trails, we take a dip.
The stardust drips from a wobbly lip,
Creating constellations where dreams flip.

Shooting past planets, we laugh and cheer,
In a race with a comet, oh so near.
The Milky Way doesn't have a steer,
While cosmic breadcrumbs lead us here.

We met a space cat with oversized paws,
Who dances with aliens and plays the saw.
Together we giggle without a pause,
In orbit around the galaxy's laws.

As we reach the end of this wacky spree,
We build a home under a glowing tree.
With cookies that sparkle, we all agree,
This odyssey's where we long to be!

Eclipsed in Metaphor

In a world where cats can fly,
Wearing hats and making pie.
They zoom across the glowing skies,
Chasing mice with starry eyes.

A dog on roller skates takes flight,
Waving at the moon so bright.
With a wink, he twirls in space,
Leaving trails of laughter's trace.

Balloons with faces dance and twirl,
While candy canes begin to swirl.
The sun sings songs of silly glee,
As unicorns sip cosmic tea.

Through metaphors we soar so high,
Playing games that twist and fly.
Each laugh a planet, round and wide,
In this universe of joy, we glide.

The Space Between Words

Words parachute like bright butterflies,
Fluttering gently beneath the skies.
Between the letters, giggles hide,
In the playground where puns abide.

A sneeze can launch a comet's tail,
While pickle hats set off a sail.
The whispers of curious dreams collide,
In every nook where rhymes reside.

Let's dance with phrases spinning free,
As jellybeans bounce in jubilee.
In this cosmos of quirky fun,
Every pun shines like the sun.

So here we float, in joyful verse,
No need to worry, no need to curse.
In the space we craft and play,
Laughter leads the way today.

Ethereal Echoes of the Universe

In the stardust, giggles form,
Creating ripples, bright and warm.
A teddy bear spins through the night,
Chasing shadows with delight.

Invisible ink writes on the stars,
While bananas float in cars.
Each echo a chuckle, firmly placed,
In the heart of this cosmic space.

Jellyfish play hopscotch with light,
Tickling the moon with sheer delight.
Shooting stars send whispers down,
Turning dreams upside down.

In this realm of silly sights,
Where giggles stretch to dizzy heights.
The echoes of laughter spread wide,
In the universe, we're all allied.

Journey into the Cosmic Heart

Let's board the boat of silly dreams,
Sailing on chocolate rivers and streams.
With marshmallow clouds that bounce and sway,
On our merry cosmic holiday.

Counting jellybeans on a star,
As wacky creatures dance afar.
Each twist and turn a giggling spark,
In the fun zone of the cosmic park.

We'll tickle comets, grab a wink,
In the universe where nonsense links.
With every ha-ha and every cheer,
The cosmic heart beats bright and clear.

So raise your cups of soda pop,
Toast to the laughter, never stop!
On this journey, hold on tight,
For every rhyme is pure delight.

Galactic Elixirs

In a jar made of stars, I found a brew,
A splash of Martian mud, just for you.
Pour it over some moon cheese, oh what a sight,
Tastes just like rubber, but feels so light.

Jupiter's juice, it's fizzy and bright,
Twinkling with flavors, oh what a delight.
Sipping and giggling, we float like a cloud,
Drinking cosmic sodas, feeling quite proud.

Saturn's ring donuts, covered in sprinkles,
They fly off the table, with quick little twinkles.
Catch them with laughter, as they zoom by,
Each bite is a chuckle, oh my oh my!

With space snacks surrounding, our party's in flight,
We'll dance with the comets, till morning's first light.
Joy in the cosmos, there's nothing to fear,
In the laughter of planets, we cheer and we cheer.

Planetary Prose

On Venus, the clouds have candy galore,
Each fluff is a marshmallow, isn't that pure?
We hop from one cloud to another with glee,
Sugar-coated skies, come and dine with me!

Mercury's heat, we try to stay cool,
But laughing at sunburns makes us feel like fools.
Shady spots playing hide-and-seek with the rays,
Who knew sunlight could spark such clumsy plays?

Neptune's blue oceans are simply divine,
Swimming in bubbles that burst with a whine.
We belly flop down, with splashes and grins,
Sailing through laughter, this is where fun begins!

With tales from the cosmos, we gather around,
Sharing our giggles; oh aren't we spellbound?
In this literary space, we soar high and wide,
Writing our stories, with joy as our guide.

The Expansive Infinity

In the void where the giggles begin to swell,
Echoes of chuckles ring like a bell.
Stars flash their smiles through the dark of the night,
As we're floating in laughter, it's pure delight.

Comets are racing in a silly parade,
Each tail full of joy, never will it fade.
With a wink and a grin, they twirl through the skies,
A dance of our dreams with silly surprise.

The asteroids roll like big bowling balls,
Landing with plops, making funny calls.
Oh, watch out! Here comes a cosmic split,
As we roll with the punches, never will quit.

Infinity stretches with our playful spree,
With each goofy joke, we're soaring so free.
In this vast universe, where fun is our tweak,
We'll laugh through the ages, so bright, so unique!

Beyond the Starline

Past the twinkling lights where the giggles are grand,
We voyage together, two friends hand in hand.
With stardust confetti that tickles our nose,
And laughter erupts like a blooming rose.

Out here in the cosmos, where silliness reigns,
We'll ride on the tails of the comet's fast trains.
Sipping on starlight, with chocolate moons too,
Chasing down chuckles like we always do.

Planets all wobble to the beats we create,
As we spin through the galaxy, feeling just great.
In each swirling orbit, we discover our glee,
Beyond the starline, forever we'll be.

So here's to the laughter that brightens our way,
In the vast endless night, we're here here to stay.
With each tickle of humor, our spirits will soar,
In this playground of dreams, who could ask for more?

Universal Chants

Zooming past the stars so bright,
A squirrel spins out of sheer delight.
With tiny bells on every tail,
They giggle on their cosmic trail.

They wear their hats made of cheese,
Floating high on lunar breeze.
As they twirl and take a chance,
They lead the universe in dance!

The planets join, in line they wait,
A galactic worm will be their mate.
They partner up in silly spins,
Creating chaos, giggles win!

Upon a comet, they'll set balls,
With jellybeans and giggly calls.
Together they make quite a show,
In space where all the laughter flows.

Spacebound Sonnets

An alien chef stirs soup with glee,
Made of stardust and a strange green pea.
His apron sparkles as he brews,
With flavors that give Martians the blues.

While comets race and rockets zoom,
His special dish fills the empty room.
With laughter ringing, they take a sip,
"More moon cheese!"—they share a nibble and quip.

Galaxies pooled in a wine glass high,
Sipping starlight, oh my, oh my!
Confetti bursts from the Milky Way,
Celebrating with a wild ballet.

Each twinkling star joins in the fun,
Chasing dreams till the night is done.
In the cosmos, a feast awaits,
With joy and laughter on all plates!

Milky Way Musings

Zany space cows float on by,
Mooing softly to the sky.
With rocket boots, they take their pace,
In search of the best grazing space.

The stars become their shining guide,
Bouncing along the cosmic tide.
They twirl through rings of Saturn's dress,
Mooing songs of space, nothing less!

Silly chicks in bright pink hats,
Launch from Jupiter and land with splats.
They sing to Mars with funny beats,
Dancing on their teeny feet.

In this dance of the milky way,
Laughter lights up every day.
With each twinkle, a joke mounts,
Space, oh space, what fun it counts!

Asteroid Anthems

Asteroids gather for a jam,
Strumming strings with no big slam.
They rock and roll with a mighty cheer,
While space dust dances, far and near.

A purple one begins to sing,
With notes that make the galaxies swing.
"Join us, friends!" the comets shout,
As bouncing meteors twist about!

The laughter floats on solar rays,
With echoes of their goofy plays.
They tap their rocks and clap their hands,
Creating rhythms through the lands!

So bounce and sway, watch them all,
In the void, they're having a ball.
A cosmic party filled with cheer,
Asteroids jamming, far and near!

Verses in the Vortex of Time

In a whirl of giggles, we spin and sway,
Time takes a twist, in a funny way.
Laughter is fuel, we zoom in delight,
Chasing the seconds, with all of our might.

Socks on our heads, we dance in the air,
Tick-tock, tick-tock, forget all your care.
Jumping through moments like bouncing balloons,
Who knew that time could be such a boon?

Ribbons of time tied in knots at our feet,
Wiggling freely, we shuffle and cheat.
Each giggle a star, brightening the night,
We're lost in the fun, what a curious sight!

So, come join our vortex, let's spin in the glow,
Time's just a game, come on, let's go!

The Dreamers' Flight across the Cosmos

Up in the air with dreams full of cheer,
We soar through the stars without any fear.
With cupcakes for rockets and cookies for fuel,
We voyage through stardust, oh, isn't it cool?

A moon made of cheese, we'll nibble and snack,
Dancing on planets, we'll never look back.
Frogs in tuxedos, they leap by our side,
What a strange crew for this cosmic ride!

Jellybean meteors fall from the sky,
We giggle and catch them as they zoom by.
Floating on laughter, we tickle the stars,
Dreamers and gigglers, just traveling far!

So, grab your imagination and let's take flight,
In our whimsical journey through the cosmic night!

Poetic Paths to the Planets

On paths paved with rhymes, to planets we'll go,
With giggles like rockets, we'll put on a show.
Each step made of verses, we skip and we hop,
Dancing through stardust, we'll never stop!

Jupiter jumpsuits, Saturn's swings too,
Mercury's merry-go-round's waiting for you.
With comets for candy, we'll share a sweet treat,
Moonbeams for ice cream, oh, isn't it neat?

We'll wander past Venus, in glittery shoes,
Playing with wishes, we'll never lose.
Galactic giggles, the best kind of sound,
Exploring this universe, joy knows no bound!

So, come take a stroll down our rhyming way,
To planets and poetry, come join the play!

Starborne Serenades

Under the blanket of twinkling cheer,
We'll serenade stars, can you hear?
With melodies silly and lyrics so bright,
Our voices will soar and sparkle in the night.

A saxophone asteroid, a banjo so round,
Join our space band, we've got laughter unbound.
Cosmic hiccups and giggles divine,
Dance with the moons, feel the rhythm align!

We'll sing to the planets, a jolly old tune,
Jiving with comets that shimmer like June.
Our symphony splendid, oh, what a delight,
Starborne in laughter, we'll fill up the night!

So come join our concert of joy on the air,
In the vastness of space, we'll dance without care!

Moonlight Melodies in Space

In the night, stars take flight,
Juggling comets, what a sight!
Planets dance in cosmic trance,
Saturn's rings spin with a prance.

Aliens wear hats made of cheese,
Wobbling 'round with silly ease.
Meteor showers, popcorn flies,
Laughter bursts in starlit skies.

Galaxies play a tune so bright,
Singing songs of pure delight.
Each note drips like moonlit dew,
Join the fun, there's room for you!

Bouncing off the Milky Way,
Space cats play, oh what a day!
With cosmic dice, they roll and cheer,
In their games, there's no more fear.

A Symphony of Celestial Bodies

In the void, a band appears,
Playing tunes that bring us cheers.
Planets strum on space guitars,
Dancing under glittering stars.

A comet taps a funky beat,
While asteroids shuffle their feet.
Uranus joins with a sly grin,
And Venus bursts out with a spin.

Shooting stars throw sparks of fun,
As laughter echoes, everyone!
Even the sun wants to sway,
To this rhythm from afar away.

Galactic friends in a grand parade,
With moonbeams shining, never fade.
Join the concert, don't be shy,
Together, we'll reach for the sky!

Rhymes in the Realm of Glimmering Stars

Upon a moonbeam, rhymes are spun,
Where giggles float and dances run.
Twinkling tales of silly sights,
Lunar lollipops and candy flights.

Stars trade jokes in outer space,
With giggles that cannot be replaced.
Cosmic doughnuts zoom on by,
Sprinkled with stardust, oh my, my!

Satellites sing a harmony,
Of wacky stars and banter free.
Silly shadows laugh and play,
Wishing on wishes without delay.

In this realm, jesters twirl,
While comets in wigs begin to whirl.
Join the laughter, take a ride,
In this space where giggles abide.

Galactic Strokes of Imagination

Brush a cloud with colors bright,
As nebulae dance with delight.
Galaxies swirl in creative flow,
Painting dreams, what a show!

Starfish sketch with glowing pens,
Creating friends that never end.
Saturn draws with rings so round,
Whimsical wonders abound, abound!

Asteroids chip in with their flair,
Crafting stories beyond compare.
In this studio of the skies,
Imagination truly flies.

So gather 'round, both young and old,
Unleash your dreams, let them unfold.
In cosmic art, we all can play,
Creating joy in a vibrant way!

Dreamscapes in Expanse of Stars

Zooming through the galaxy, oh what a sight,
Aliens juggling planets, under the moonlight.
They invite me to dance on the rings of a star,
With my wacky space boots, I twirl near and far.

Floating on comets, like ice cream in space,
I'm chased by a space cat, oh what a race!
He wears a fine suit, and he offers me cheese,
While gravity laughs, and the cosmos just wheezes.

We build made of stardust, a house up on Mars,
With a sign made of sparkles, "Welcome to Ours!"
We sip fizzy stardust from glasses that shine,
And toast to the giggles in a universe divine.

As I drift back to Earth, my journey feels bright,
With laughter and joy, oh what a delight!
In dreamscapes of stardust, where silliness glows,
I scribble my stories, where imagination flows.

The Nebula's Narrative

In the tale of a nebula, colors collide,
A skunk in a spacesuit, put on a wild ride.
He's spinning and twirling, with a grin on his face,
Squirting out laughter, in a cosmic embrace.

The stars gather 'round for a comedic show,
Chortling and chuckling, in a bright cosmic glow.
"Why don't aliens play hide-and-seek?" they sigh,
"Because they can't find their ships when they fly!"

A cow on a rocket, what a sight to behold,
Mooing stardust wishes, both new and retold.
With a wink and a whim, they all take to flight,
In the nebula's narrative, everything's light.

The curtain of darkness pulls back with a smile,
"Join us for laughter, come stay for a while!"
As the universe chuckles, in giggles and beams,
These whimsical moments are all of our dreams.

Starward Bound in Rhyme

A spaceship with wings, oh what a delight,
It dives through the asteroids, ducks left and right.
Pilots in pajamas, drinking space lemonade,
They laugh and they giggle, as they zoom and parade.

One wobbly astronaut, slips on his shoe,
Sails past a starfish who giggles, "Woohoo!"
With tumbling planets rolling off in a spin,
They bounce off each other, just let the fun begin!

With glittering trails, we paint the night sky,
A comet's a painter, who loves to fly high.
It splashes the cosmos with colors so bright,
Each stroke brings a chuckle, a whimsical sight.

Bound for adventure, our journey's a blast,
With jokes and with gaffes, we're up and we're fast.
In this starward escapade, silliness reigns,
With giggles in orbit, fun never wanes.

The Universe Whispers Poetry

The universe whispers, a rhyme in the breeze,
Stars giggle and twinkle, just doing as they please.
With pulsing electric, the cosmos unfurls,
It's a concert of planets, oh what fun twirls!

A cheeky black hole, with secrets so deep,
Sings lullabies softly, coaxing us to sleep.
But wait! There's a dance with a moon so round,
Wobbling and bobbing, in joy they astound.

Aliens recite their own silly verse,
About a lost spaceship that went on a course,
It's wedged in a donut, "Help me!" they cry,
With laughter echoing, the stars wink and sigh.

The universe whispers, with joy in each line,
Painting laughter and giggles through space and through time.
In this whimsical realm, poetry floats free,
With chuckles of stardust, it's pure jubilee!

Horizons Painted with Poetic Light

In a sky of pink and green,
The weirdest birds have been seen.
They wear their socks all mismatched,
And sing in tunes that are quite hatched.

With a wink and a flying leap,
They tell stories that make you sheep.
Twisting tales of wobbly flight,
In the glow of the moon's delight.

As the stars begin to dance,
They prance and jig in a funny stance.
Laughter echoes through the void,
With every giggle, joy's deployed.

And if you look up in the night,
You might catch a giggle in flight.
Horizons bright with silly sights,
In this realm of starry lights.

Odes Under the Celestial Canopy

Beneath the blanket of twinkling stars,
Dance the comets, zoom in cars.
They toss about their cosmic dreams,
In a ballet of laughter and beams.

A moonbeam plays the silly flute,
While asteroids don a funny suit.
Singing songs of big and small,
In a cosmic concert, they enthrall.

With every twinkle, there's a grin,
As galaxies spin and spin.
They hold a party for all to see,
Where humor flows like zero G.

So join the jive beneath the night,
Where every joke takes flight.
With giggles echoing through the vast,
These odes are funny, unsurpassed.

Fables from the Fringes of Space

Out where the stars start to wane,
Duck-billed aliens sing a refrain.
They ride on beams of vibrant light,
Spreading giggles across the night.

With tales of cheese from distant moons,
And dancing robots humming tunes.
They tell of laughter, glow, and cheer,
With every word, the void draws near.

A spaceship filled with giggly things,
Plays tag with planets, oh, what flings!
In this fable, joy's the game,
With silly antics, none the same.

So when the stars begin to twinkle,
Listen close, and you will crinkle.
For fables spun from cosmic air,
Are filled with laughter everywhere.

Cosmic Whispers Through Time

Time travelers in socks so grand,
Swirl through space like grains of sand.
With portals spinning, oh so bright,
They share their giggles with pure delight.

Each whisper carries a funny tale,
Of Martians riding on a snail.
They giggle, they chuckle, oh, what a sound,
As cosmic laughter swirls around.

Through ages past, and years to come,
The humor thrives, it's never glum.
In every tick, a jest unfolds,
In the tapestry, the laughter holds.

So when you gaze into the skies,
Just remember, humor never dies.
For cosmic whispers dance and play,
Bringing smiles along the way.

Starlight Chronicles

In a ship made of cheese,
We zoom through the skies,
Dodging comets and bees,
With a wink and a sigh.

Galactic cows float by,
They moo in the stars,
With googly eyes awry,
They giggle from Mars.

The planets play hide and seek,
As the sun takes a nap,
While jupiter gives a squeak,
In an oversized cap.

We dance on Saturn's rings,
In our space suits of pink,
Where all the rad things,
Are made out of blink.

Moonbeam Tales,

On a crescent moon swing,
We sway to the beat,
Of crickets that sing,
With fancy light feet.

A playful star does dip,
In a puddle of light,
And we share a quick flip,
In the giggles of night.

The cosmos unfolds a map,
Where fun never ends,
While we do a quick tap,
With our alien friends.

With laughter that glows,
We ride on moonbeams,
As the starlight flows,
And sparks all our dreams.

Ascending in Rhyme

Up, up, we rise high,
With a pop and a cheer,
Past the clouds in the sky,
Oh what fun we steer!

Each verse gives a twist,
As we spin round and round,
With a giggle, we missed,
All the laughs we found.

Asteroids dance and twirl,
As we bob and we weave,
Creating a twinkling swirl,
For the night to believe.

In a world full of glee,
Where stars wink and play,
We'll make history,
On this hilarious way.

Poetic Flare in a Nebula's Glow

In a nebula bright,
We spark with delight,
Painting tales with flair,
Through the cosmic air.

Juggling planets with glee,
In a whirlwind of fun,
With giggles from Venus,
And cheese from the sun.

Rocketing past the pins,
Of the Milky Way fair,
Where hilarity wins,
In the twinkling air.

With laughter as our guide,
We scribble our fate,
On stardust, we glide,
Creating our plate.

The Language of Starry Nights

Under diamond-studded skies,
Galaxies start to chat,
With whispers and sighs,
In their cosmic spat.

A comet makes a joke,
With a tail full of fizz,
As starlings dance and poke,
In a whimsical whiz.

Constellations all around,
Join the musical band,
Where giggles abound,
And joy fills the land.

In the language of stars,
We laugh and we rhyme,
Creating stories bright,
Through waves of pure time.

Verses from the Starfire Sea

In a boat made of candy, I sail the blue,
With gumdrop sails and a chocolate crew.
We giggle and bounce, in a jellyfish tide,
Chasing the stars where the silly fish hide.

A mermaid in slippers sings silly old tunes,
While dolphins wear hats shaped like crescent moons.
We splash and we dash, through bubbles and glee,
In a sea full of laughter, just you wait and see!

With jellybean sharks and a cola wave,
Every wave is a joke, every laugh, a rave.
The stars wink down with their spangled glow,
As we white-water slide on a rainbow below.

So join me, dear friend, on this ride of delight,
Where giggles are whispers and sparkles take flight.
In this starfire sea, let imagination run,
For a journey of joy has just begun!

Where Nebulas Sing

In a galaxy bright, where odd critters roam,
A chicken in space claims this place as her home.
With a top hat and cane, she flaps and she swings,
Dancing through stars, where the nebulas sing.

The comets are laughing, they're tickling me,
As robots do jazz in the cosmic debris.
Planetary polka, with aliens in tow,
Shaking their antennas, all putting on a show!

Green Martians in tutus, both funky and proud,
They twirl through the twinkling, a colorful crowd.
With a splash of starlight, and a sprinkle of cheer,
The universe bubbles with joy when you're here.

So float through the cosmos, let giggles abound,
In this nebula carnival, a fun place is found.
With laughter as music and joy as our king,
We'll dance through the stardust where nebulas sing!

Lyrical Launch into the Unknown

Strapped in a bubble, I fly through the air,
Surrounded by giggles and cotton candy flair.
With marshmallow rockets and gummy bear shields,
I zoom past the planets, oh, what joy it yields!

A cow with a helmet is steering my ride,
And cats in tuxedos are dancing outside.
"Hold on tight!" I scream, "As we launch through the stars!"
With bubble-wrap boosters, we'll go very far!

The Milky Way's winking, it's tickled with light,
We're spinning through stardust, a delightful sight.
Jellybeans pop as the fireflies glow,
In this lyrical flight to the places we'll go!

So let's sip on our punch made of rocket fizz drink,
With friends all around, we won't stop to think.
Adventure awaits in the void so profound,
As we drift into laughter, where fun will abound!

The Poetry of Cosmic Trails

On a comet's long tail, we weave and we spin,
With ice cream for fuel, let the fun times begin!
The stars tap their feet to the rhythm we make,
As we write little verses with sparkles to shake.

A kitten in goggles conducts with delight,
While octopus poets recite through the night.
With wishes like fireflies, we toss them around,
In this cosmic recital where giggles abound.

With a splash of confetti from Mars' candy shop,
We'll color the cosmos with smiles that won't stop.
The planets are bobbing to our silly tune,
As we dance with the comets beneath the bright moon.

So join in the jiving, let your giggles take flight,
In this poetry venture, we shine ever bright.
On the trails of the cosmos, we'll write our best tales,
In the funny adventures of cosmic trails!

Stargazer's Lullaby

In the night, the stars do twinkle,
Winking at me, with a soft sprinkle.
Space mice dance on the moon's big cheese,
They giggle and bounce in a cosmic breeze.

Dreaming of comets with curly tails,
Sailing on whispers of solar gales.
Counting the meteors, I fall asleep,
While aliens laugh, their secret to keep.

My pillow's a planet, cozy and round,
With fluffy clouds as my bedspread found.
Each pillow fight sends stardust to play,
As I join the cosmos and drift far away.

Giggles echo through the cosmic night,
While shooting stars flash, oh what a sight!
In this lullaby, the universe sings,
As sleep takes me, on fantastical wings.

The Ballad of Boundless Skies

Up in the clouds where the funny birds fly,
They wear tiny hats and wave as they pass by.
With a flap and a flap, they flutter and tease,
Showing off wings with the greatest of ease.

Bouncing on rainbows, they tumble with glee,
Chasing after sunlight, so wild and free.
The sun winks back with a golden smile,
Inviting them in for a giggly while.

Look out for shadows, it's just a big kite,
Floating along, trying to steal the daylight.
But the clouds just chuckle and puff out their chests,
"No kites allowed here, we're hosting a fest!"

So if you hear laughter from up in the blue,
It's birds playing darts with a touch of a clue.
Join them in their frolic, don't let laughter die,
For there's magic in each cloud that floats by.

Fragments of Infinity in Rhyme

In the cosmos, where giggles bloom,
Spaceships zoom past with vrooms of zoom.
Each star is a lightbulb, twinkling and bright,
Silly aliens sing, 'Oh what a night!'

Galaxies swirl like a merry-go-round,
While marshmallow meteors softly abound.
Popcorn comets burst, with flavors galore,
Want a bucket of stardust? I've got plenty more!

Twinkling tunes spin through the wide expanse,
Planets all wobble in a silly dance.
With giggles and laughter, they join the parade,
Jump up and down, it's a cosmic charade!

We're diving through stardust, on whimsy we ride,
The universe giggles, in laughter we glide.
In fragments of infinity, life's a delight,
With rhymes in the starlight, we twinkle tonight.

Wonders Beyond the Event Horizon

Past the edge where the wild things play,
Time twists and flops in a silly way.
Wormholes are whirlpools of giggles and sighs,
Where time takes a nap and the gravity flies.

Napping space cats pounce with delight,
Chasing lost time through the vast starry night.
A dance-off happens on planets of cheese,
As flying space turtles join in with ease.

Cosmic confetti rains down in a swirl,
Each speck is a wish from a giggly girl.
Twisting through stardust, we laugh at the scene,
In a galaxy far, where we've never been.

So come ride the rockets of laughter and cheer,
For wonders await 'hind the soft cosmic sphere.
Just hold on tight, as we soar and we glide,
In the universe's hug, where joy's on the ride.

Interstellar Whispers

In a tin can zooming fast,
A hamster pilot made to last.
He steers with snacks and silly tunes,
Bouncing in the starry dunes.

Asteroids bop like disco balls,
As Martians dance in cosmic halls.
With every spin and silly cheer,
They giggle loud for all to hear.

The moon plays peek-a-boo with light,
While aliens join the giggling flight.
With every laugh, the stars ignite,
A glowing giggle, oh what a sight!

In the vacuum, silly sounds float,
A chorus born from a fuzzy goat.
Who knew the cosmos had such flair?
With cosmic humor in the air!

Cosmic Verse Voyage

Bouncing comets race and play,
Juggling stars in a bright ballet.
A purple cat with polka dots,
Trips on space cheese, oh what a plot!

The sun is winking with a grin,
As meteors wear their silly skin.
With every twist and every roll,
Giggles echo through the black hole.

Planets wear their best tutus,
Bobbling up the starry blues.
They dance and spin in cosmic cheer,
Creating giggles for all to hear.

In this voyage, joy is found,
Around each star, laughter sounds.
And at the end, they all unite,
To share a laugh in cosmic light!

Astral Adventures

A space snail zooms with style and grace,
Sliding through the stars in a dizzy race.
With floppy ears and shades so bright,
He twirls and spins into the night.

Galactic frogs leap high with glee,
Playing hopscotch near a cosmic tree.
With every bounce, a giggle lands,
Creating ripples in colorful strands.

In nebulae, they celebrate,
Dancing to music that feels just great.
With glittering lights like candy bars,
They jump for joy amongst the stars.

When asteroids start a silly fight,
The laughter echoes with sheer delight.
It's hard to frown in this grand space fair,
Where funny moments float in the air!

Galaxy Rhythms

In a dance-off on Saturn's rings,
Aliens show off wacky swings.
With every move, they crack a joke,
And twirl around like funky smoke.

Stars wink as they share funny tales,
Of flying boats and silly snails.
With laughter echoing far and wide,
They ride the comets on a wild slide.

The sun bursts out in chuckles bright,
Lighting up the velvety night.
Planets giggle with every spin,
Creating joy from deep within.

So come aboard this silly ride,
Where laughter soars and stars collide.
In the galaxy of goofy dreams,
The cosmic fun is bursting at the seams!

Lyrics of the Luminous Void

In a capsule of cheese, we zoom through the sky,
Chasing pizza-shaped clouds, oh my, oh my!
Aliens tap-dance on Saturn's wide rings,
While we laugh and cheer, and dance on soft springs.

With a slingshot of laughter, we pilot our craft,
Dodging asteroids shaped like a big silly giraffe.
Stars wink and giggle, as we whirl and spin,
Galaxy's got jokes, let the fun times begin!

We play tag with comets, zoom fast then slow,
Sharing punchlines with Venus, the glowing show.
Cosmic confetti falls, what a glittery sight,
We party through the cosmos, in pure delight.

Hitchhiking on beams of bright moonlight's glow,
Collecting space treasures in a jar we stow.
At the edge of the universe, we take a big sigh,
Silly dreams go zooming, just soaring on high!

Echoes from the Edge of the Universe

Riding waves of sound, we squeak and we squeal,
Finding galactic fish that dance and reel.
With giggles that echo in the vastness of space,
We pull pranks on the stars, with a wink and a chase.

We wear space helmets covered in glittery foam,
Juggling moons like planets, feeling right at home.
Wormholes play tricks, and spin us around,
While the asteroids laugh, making silly sounds.

A trampoline bounce on a comet's bright tail,
Shooting for Saturn, we leave a shiny trail.
Echoes of laughter ricochet and weave,
As we frolic through orbits, who dares to believe?

To the edge of forever, we set our sights wide,
With a wink to the cosmos, we'll giggle and glide.
The universe winks back, with stars shining bright,
In a carnival of fun, we dance through the night.

Stanzas of the Stardust Voyage

On a ship made of candy, we sail 'cross the night,
Chasing dreams in the cosmos, all sparkly and bright.
Jellybean asteroids bounce off our course,
While stardust rains down, pure cosmic remorse.

With a hiccup of laughter, we twist and we twirl,
Space whales sing ballads, as we give them a whirl.
Galaxies giggle, with a sparkle and gleam,
As we dance through the stardust, lost in a dream.

We hiccup through nebulae, colors collide,
In the blink of a supernova, we cheekily slide.
Tickling a comet, it shoots us on by,
As we burst into laughter, echoing high.

From the farthest of realms, we spin and we sigh,
Crafting memories bright, like candy on high.
With starlit confetti, we aim for the sky,
On this voyage of wonder, we carefree fly!

Journeying Through Celestial Sonnets

In a bubble of joy, we float past the moons,
Sing songs to the asteroids, dancing in tunes.
With marshmallow clouds, we surf on the breeze,
Butterflies of starlight, we chase with such ease.

In the rhythm of comets, we spin without care,
Sharing giggles with meteors zooming to share.
Lights from the planets form a disco of glee,
As we dance through the cosmos, so wild and so free.

Whispers of space winds, they tickle our cheeks,
Charming little comets, oh how the fun speaks!
We play hide and seek with the stars big and small,
Every twinkle a giggle, the universe's call.

On a journey so silly, we soar through the skies,
With a wink and a nod, leave the mundane behind.
In the laughter of light, our joy intertwines,
Exploring the cosmos, where silliness shines!

www.ingramcontent.com/pod-product-compliance
Lightning Source LLC
Chambersburg PA
CBHW051639160426
43209CB00004B/715